Recordings of Dead Languages

Recordings of Dead Languages

poems

Chad Heltzel

Chicago | Los Angeles

Published in the United States by Match Factory Editions, 2025

ISBN 978-1-966253-16-7 (hardcover)
ISBN 978-1-966253-15-0 (paperback)
ISBN 978-1-966253-17-4 (ebook)

Library of Congress Control Number: 2025933433

matchfactoryeditions.com

Book layout by RD Morgan

Cover art and design by Gretchen Hasse

Colophon design by Randy Cochran

TABLE OF CONTENTS

I. CURRENT

II. THE HUNTER'S MOON OVER CHICAGO

III. ARCHAEOACOUSTICS

I. CURRENT

Natural History

Precambrian to Cenozoic: volcanoes emerging
from prehistoric seas; green algae spewing from vents
on the ocean floor; the lineage of arthropods,
brachiopods, ancient fish, ferns and pines;
the Ice Age and evolution of giant bears, lions, elephants.
As the earth broke apart, animals traveled bridges
of quaking land, were stranded on archipelagoes
caused from the breakage. At the mural's end,
the escalator rises to the ceiling like a stalagmite,
and all the passengers make their way from underground cars
to the rail line above the street. We are still crossing.

Recognition

Eleven new species discovered
in a central Vietnam mountain rainforest:
three species of rare leafless orchids.
One produces a black flower. Also, a butterfly,
yellow-striped with red spots
along the body—a skipper, quickly darting
when it flies. Only a decade ago,
a new species of wild cattle was found roaming
here among the trees: nothing so small
as insect or flower: in the country's heart,
somehow lost to sight. And all this time,
the river has provided its water
for thousands living downstream.
It is called the Perfume River, no less—
its scent gathered from tropical flora
growing along its banks after traveling
through fifty-five waterfalls.

Follow it: mock lemon, cinnamon bark,
lotus flower that creates tea from its water.
Gardenia, camellia, cilantro—the river pocking with rain
dripping off the epiphytes. Here is where
you find it. In the blurred distance,
a crow waits indifferently between a shimmer
either tombstone or flood pool. Ribbons of water hoses,
red and blue, lead to the grave site.
The water has gathered inside,
blankets the floor of the hole.
At a glimpse, it is all there,
but only for a second. Everything is here.

Urchins and starfish. Rupture of light.
Water drops. Vanilla bean.
Mother and father. Black orchid.

Tell the Bees

I saw a bee issue from the mouth of my sleeping friend.

In the coffin, place a bowl on the deceased's chest. To hold pins.

Country people apply rotten fruit mold to their wounds.

Plato says quiet souls come to life as bees.

During a lightning storm, drape the mirrors. In the presence of death, drape the mirrors.

The bee left her mouth, entered an abandoned building's bricks.

When she dies, tell the child to visit the hives.

In her dream, she crossed a silver bridge to a treasure-filled palace.

Tie a black crepe to the hive. Tap on it with a chain of keys.

Whisper three times: <...>

The bees will come to the funeral. Find one among the pins.

After the End of the World: Centos

1.

Each of them would soon be
an island in an archipelago of drained time.
On their backs were vermiculate patterns
that were maps of the world in its becoming.
The illusion of depth, created by a frame,
the arrangement of shapes on a flat surface.
Her concern with landscapes and living creatures
was passionate. Her first narcissi were in bloom,
and the daffodils behind them were already
showing flower buds. It is said there are flowers
that bloom only once in a hundred years. Why
should there not be some that bloom once
in a thousand, in ten thousand years?

There were men, even before his time,
who caught glimpses of the shadow.
Pursued by strange visions, he would never
carve another piece of wood or play the violin,
a second Adam searching for the forgotten
paradises of the reborn sun. There are souls,
he thought, whose umbilicus has never been cut.
He had kissed another dead face only
a few days before, but centuries lay between
the two salutations.

She leaned out and looked past the mills
to the hills. What will the mind do, each morning,
waking? *You have nothing. You possess nothing.*

You own nothing. You are free. It was strange,
she thought, that it should require a holocaust
to make her own life worth living.

It was some time later that he failed to notice it had started to rain.

2.

The surface of the water turned to fire.
The cells floating into the air like sparks
from a campfire. Dense palls of opaque gas
swirled across the sky, poured over us, filtering
into our bodies, minds, hearts, into the pavement itself.
Once again the atmosphere lightened. The physics had changed.
We lived in the blank white spaces at the edges.
It seemed sensible to crave safety, to crave
shelter from the bombs and the birds and the daily
depravity of war. It seemed like we were holding onto
each other because that was the only way to stop us
being swept away into the night. We were,
on that day, no different from the ancients.
We collected all the bones we could find,
we wrote the truest, simplest things we knew—
our names, the date, and these words: *We were here.*

3.

On the white beach, ground-up coral and broken
bones; a group of the children are waking.
Now at this hour, when the cirrus clouds stretched
like crimson ribbons high across the southwest sky,
she wanted to feel love the way a bone feels
a break. Love doesn't just sit there, like a stone;
it has to be made, like bread.
A loaf of bread with an arrow stuck in it.

Pain was a fascinating horror.
It's so heartbreaking, violence, when it's in a house—
like seeing the clothes in a tree after an explosion.

A quarter of a century later, the two brothers stood
together. They never went back to the clearing
in the wood. Children are always ready to believe
that adult catastrophes are their fault.
As sometimes happens, a death healed a family breach.

4.

To survive atrocity is to be made an honorary consul
to a republic of pain. We all have our harps to play,
saw a new world coming rapidly—
something not life, long, stretching out endless.
But when the world became bright with reason
and riches, it began to sense the narrowness of
the needle's eye. History had a slow pulse.
Everything is imprinted forever with what it once was.
Suddenly I was trapped. My hair was grey,
fixed in a sort of eternity at the heart of the crystal.
Night falls. Or has fallen. Is hard to remember
afterwards, like pain. And then the lights were back
so quickly that it was like a hallucination.

5.

All those cities, all those fields and farms,
with nobody, and nothing left alive.
The avocados are caving in
on themselves, the peaches developing sinking brown
craters like eyes. This orangeless world.
Not only the portraits on the walls, but also
the shelves in the library were thinned out.
Ground to dust and plowed with salt.
I felt the weakness of these books, their immateriality, how
they had failed to change the world. I want
everything back, the way it was. But there is
no point to it, this wanting.

You saw the foundations of the world.
And they were solid. Here I stand. But no longer
with my words, brilliantly alone. There was a wall.
It did not look important. It was built
of uncut rocks roughly mortared.
I'm going to go unbuild walls.

I would take from the ground some of the blue-white
poison that makes statues of men. And then,
with all the forests being killed and all the lakes
being poisoned by acid rain, on a day meaninglessly
close to the present one, meaninglessly like
the present one, I would disappear from the earth.
If your soul left this earth, I would follow and find you.

Pastoral

On the roadside billboard:
Jesus is real. Little maples are growing
in the collapsing farmhouse gutters,
In the front yard, a tulip
tree struck by lightning.
One half white. Termites burrowed under
the house and into the living room,
consumed a shelf of encyclopedias.
No more moas, no money, no mythologies.
The television: *One in four mammals*
will soon be extinct. This year, the fields
are surprisingly green. Everything—
the beans, the corn, the maples, the pigweed—
all deep emerald green. The other side:
Hell is real. And the fields. All one green.

A Brief History of Extinction

Ile aux Aigrettes, off the coast of Mauritius,
harbors endangered species of ebony.
A pink pigeon lives here. It was once home
to its own species of tortoise,
now extinct. In its place,
the Aldabra giant tortoise has been introduced
to fill its niche. A dodo statue stands in the forest
as a memorial to the island's history of extinction.
Upon its discovery, the dodo was classified
as a type of swan, or vulture, or albatross. The island
Ile aux Aigrettes means Island of Egrets. There are
no native egrets here; only the cattle egret is found here,
an accidental species blown by typhoons, lost
on its course. The dodo was in fact
a giant pigeon, and its closest living relative
is the nicobar pigeon, named for its jade green gizzard stone,
used to make jewelry. Elsewhere in Mauritius,
fossils of dodos and other recently extinct animals
were unearthed from the marshland of Mare aux Songes,
where treasure seekers continue to hunt for pirates'
buried riches. The dodo bones found in the marsh
are now on display at Oxford University.
Other museums possess a head, a foot, a fragment.
We have yet to process the effect of its loss.
Consider the tambalacoque. Its age is impossible to determine
as it bears no growth rings. The tree goes by many names:
calvaria, dodo tree, *Sideroxylon grandiflorum*
(once *Calvaria major*). Note: names change over time.
As more species become known, we must find
more names. If the species fits better elsewhere,

it should be renamed. In the 1970s,
scientists believed only thirteen specimens of tambalacoque
had survived the centuries. A study concluded
the trees' hard seeds must have been broken
by the gizzards of dodos: since the dodo had been extinct
for over two hundred years, the trees could not
germinate without passage through the birds.
In fact, new trees have grown:
saplings are difficult to identify, are often confused
with other species. Botanists can germinate the seeds
by force-feeding them to turkeys or tumbling them
in gem polishers, turning them into jewels. Today,
Dodo is a brand of jewelry. Ads feature
a panning shot of ocean-blue waters
above coral reefs. Nouveau riche youth surf and drink wine
in a sailboat. Charms are available in the shapes
of seahorses, octopuses, starfish. Bestsellers include
Summer Woman, More Love, Follow Your Dreams.

Current

In the field through which the observer walks—
the black boot of one standing as if to measure
the opening of the other's mouth, having come up for air
to breathe forever and die that way, these giants wash ashore
and waste to bone on the beach, a smooth path
worn into sand by their fins, as the surf's rinse
relieves the pain of their organs crushing
under their bodies' weight— perhaps all of this
is a question of the magnetic field— there must be
an invisible eddy projected from the Earth's core
through which all things drift, and from that current
comes a sudden flow of tremors pulling the compass
apart, conducting the field of whales toward coastline
gently enough to move them with salt's buoyancy
and yet with such force to compel
their immensity out of the ocean—the act of flowing become flux,
as change in the nature of breath, for example—
such that oxygen inside the body becomes new
through an act of intimacy—a molecule of air propelled
from pockets in the lungs, the stream charging
from neuronal pathways, rushing along synapses
like electricity passing through coils
in waves of sparking light, like waves of water
produced by the submarine drifting of plates—
the Earth's interior heating, then funneling upward
through mountains created by colliding masses—
so hot even iron, able to change properties in the path of the field,
loses its power—so high the waves reach fifty feet
and plow into the seaside, a wall of water inundating
runners in the tide's crush, drowning them at sea

among the timber of their homes—
and so many miles away, the whales drift up
on the opposite shore of a continent, lying on their sides,
trying to right themselves at my feet.

Dust Storm

In this empty lot, starlings fly along
the edge of a giant dust cloud that swallows
sheets of paper and sweeps the grass
poking through cracked concrete.
As the funnel swirls, the birds
grip its boundary in air, then land briefly,
rising and descending in waves:
a shroud of drapery to cover buildings,
or a dress loosening from the shoulder,
before falling in folds to the ground.
Like Hokusai's woodcut: rising whitecaps
in the image of Mount Fuji, curls of water
dropping gulls into a bamboo forest,
in circles. Then a pool of blackness,
birds again. Birds as water,
or dust: living things
peel and fall from the storm.

Fragments of North Carolina

1. From the First Night

Sleeping, dreaming of waking,
my father's house. Eleven o'clock
in the morning and the sky is night-dark,
the stars still visible. In the distance,
funnel clouds descend into a field.
I know this is my father's house,
that he is absent from it.
Outside, in the warm spring air,
snow falls, the white gathering on hedgerows.
Lightning gains momentum,
runs between clouds: handwriting.
Dying at Earth's end
in a home in want of its owner.

2. Wilmington

Spring: sun gleams through the drapes
into the bedroom. In the yard,
a green butterfly probes a foxglove.
Through a Japanese maple's blossoms,
a row of evergreens. My watch,
its battery replaced almost a year ago, stops;
the digital numbers ticking off seconds
fade away. Elsewhere, live oaks are in bloom.
They shed green strands of pollen,
their chartreuse film soon to be pulverized
into the concrete. Some hornets land in the swimming pool.
They float, occasionally kick the water's skim.

A drowned woman was buried
in the cemetery downtown. A spy
for the Confederacy, she died
in a naval attack off the coast,
rescuing heavy bags of gold
falling with the ship's mass.
Soldiers rescued her weighted body
from the water, and the boat
burned into the sea, forming a barrier reef.

3. Fragments of North Carolina

With a metal detector, one can find buttons
from soldiers' coats, unexploded bombs
from the Civil War. In museums,
speakers tell stories of those whose possessions
lie encased behind glass: *Here is a broken telescope.*
Some playing cards. A fragment of a bottle.
A vial of raisins imported from Greece, completely desiccated.
In the aquarium, another voice describes
the New River: *The second oldest in the world,*
flowing down the Appalachians from Virginia,
draining into the Atlantic. Here, an artificial reef
including the semblance of coral,
a room full of whale bones, a jaw large enough
to fit a human body inside.
Outside, what remains intact: an ocean's estuary
empties into a pond surrounded by a line of sea oats,
one wild duck floating in its center.
Farther, below the grove of live oaks
lining the dunes, the war's excavated bunkers.
Given the right tools, we could find
our ancestors' remains underneath,
their belongings when they died.
In the dried seaweed blown into the burrows,
a nest of beach fleas. A whelk shell, hollowed.

4. Wakes

We leave Wilmington
on the Southport Ferry. Since the city expanded,
several bodies, discarded in hopes of never being found,
have been unearthed. In low tide,
one can walk a thin sandbar
to an island where a hermit lived for years,
sheltered under tarpaulins. Eventually,
a stranger bringing food discovered him,
murdered over a land dispute.
The island now bears his name.

My stepmother shows it to me
as the ferry stirs the water;
a sailboat rises and falls in its wake.
The water ripples, holds the smaller boat
in the waves, angles away,
changes shape. Our ferry would fill
the wakes of tugboats and cargo ships,
just as it envelops
and transforms other boats in its wash.
A cyclist with a prosthetic leg
looks over the side, watching cormorants bob along
the little whitecaps and fly onto buoys.
At the ferry's edge, a protective rope
and thick line of rust mark where sea spray
has corroded the metal.
A father and son stand there, holding hands.

5. The Pines

Towards the airport, the end of the visit.
The land is being cleared, and I ask why,
when there are so many beautiful trees.
I point my finger in a circle
to forests of long-leaf pines
lining the highway. My father says
these trees' branches crack during storms,
fall and barricade the roads. The sap
drips turpentine onto cars, eats paint.
Off a Raleigh interstate, a white heron
emerges from a clearing in the trees,
its legs stained rust
from clay dirt and dried needles.
It is perfectly still.

When the plane ascends,
I look out the window and see nothing
but the pines. The pilot tells us
there will be turbulence,
and I feel my body drop
in the seat, imagine falling thousands
of feet into the trees. The trees
breaking the fall. The break
of my body returning
to its place in the earth.

Plans

Tomorrow, my mother will fly
to Los Angeles, and she has sent me
her flight plans, numbers of people to call
if something happens. But I am
watching a blackbird fly through the library,
seeing it soar to the ceiling, above the hollow arc
of staircases, until it eventually perches
on a carrel near mine. We study each other:
its black eye darting up and back to my eye,
its feathers shining under the fluorescent light,
and then it flies away into the book stacks.
Some say a bird flying in a room
is a harbinger of death: a loved one's car
crashing, a heart failing. Yet today
will be the year's last snow:
April's tulips and daffodils dusted white.

Of Stone

Inside the gate, the grass is thick with bluebonnets
and coreopsis. The cemetery is decayed,
but not abandoned. Some new graves
have been formed in the past few years,
tin markers pushed into the dirt in front.
The ground above has not been leveled, the bodies
improperly buried. Into the piles,
visitors have placed silk flowers; above one grave,
false leaves glitter to look like fresh dew. To the side,
there is a mound into which the remains
of old silk flowers and broken stones have been thrown:
a compost that will never decompose,
will never break into mulch to cover
the bodies of the fresh dead.
Most of the graves here are over fifty years old.
Some of the markers are metal cylinders
in the shape of a body. Their engravings have worn
away. In the back of the cemetery,
headstones have toppled to the ground, fallen backwards,
and broken. China's Great Wall, too,
has begun to collapse. A farmer nearby
used its bricks to construct a pen
for his pigs. Visitors every year crush
the clay underneath their feet; its weight
cannot stand. As holes form and weaken
the wall, satellite pictures confirm
it cannot be seen from space. And here,
flowers grow through the cracks of worn
metal and stone. A cactus blooms over another.
Make no stone to commemorate my death;

let nothing mark the time
it will take for the flesh to fall from my bones.

Building a Bonfire

Sliced branches drop into heaps
of their own dust, and we carve them

into smaller pieces with a chainsaw.
We toss them in two piles: one for the living,

oak and maple leaves still attached, evergreen
needles still bound to the wood;

one for the dead limbs covered
in grey-blue scales, rotten holes

in the centers of each branch.
We stack some of the dead branches

into a fire ring, douse them
with lighter fluid, strike a match.

A hill leads down to a cornfield. October:
the harvest finished, the field is reduced

to a sea of broken reeds.
The fire begins. We gather our canvas

chairs and arrange them in a half-moon.
I cannot take my eyes from the flames.

As I watch the fire, the wind suddenly blows cold
against my neck. The crabapples drop their fruit

on the front lawn. They too will come down, soon.
From the flames, a thousand fireflies vanish.

Field Guides

Leaves fall from an opened book: novels
become field guides. Between pages five and six,
the American mountain ash: a full branch a bookmark,
and an orange berry pressed into the page
where something has smeared.
The word must have been "cruel,"
or perhaps "crucial."

The eastern redcedar: the pith carefully sliced
with a pocketknife. The center
is called heartwood. Light red in color.
The scent is legible still.
Common winterberry holly: the edges of the leaves
sharp saw-teeth, the red berries once poisonous.
They still may be: the pages above and below
permanently stained, the words unsafe to read.

In the table of contents,
sugar maple: on this one,
the color becomes gradually redder
towards the center, the edges yellow-to-orange.
As if the fingerprint's pressure
had dried into the leaves.

The Latent Image

A brief exposure of light is believed to act on some silver halide crystals in a way that produces an aggregate of metallic silver atoms. This aggregate is the latent image, the invisible building blocks from which the visible image is formed. ... Even with the best modern technology, it remains impossible to detect a latent image by direct physical or chemical means.—John Hannavy, *Encyclopedia of Nineteenth Century Photography, Volume 1*

Grand Canyon Triptych

Miles of rock and sky
to capture. A caravan
of photographers crosses
Grand Canyon trails
with a mobile darkroom.
Horses carry on their backs
cameras, plates,
musical instruments
turned sinks and tanks,
containers of liquids.
These mountain roads
have no rails;
the animals' burdens shift
over the projections.
The weight is too
much to hold:
a horse falls over.
Camera smashes.
A silver bath
rains over everything.
Shards on
the rocks. Imagine—
the dead animal
broken in the gorge,
covered with splinters

and dust. The image
at first lies invisible
on the plate.
Silver salts climb
chemical lattice works;
metal and liquid helices
converge through exposure
to light. Chlorine mist
attaches to silver crystals,
proves the permanence
of the wreckage.
The finished plate
is too delicate to touch.

On a mountainside,
a worker attaches
telephone wire
to a post. An invisible
hand readies to pull
the silhouette,
holding onto a length of string,
from the outcrop.
What appears to be
a giant's shadow
covers the opposite flank.
A dry river runs
between the giant and
man holding string.
They face each other
and have no faces.
In color, and with
moisture in the air,
a rainbowed halo called glory
will form around
the worker's shadow
and project over the sun.
Calls will come through
the wires; dust and cable
carry messages
over the trails.
Trail, incidentally,
also means shadow:
our face, its face.

Tourists watched the sun set.
A man climbed
to the peak of an outcrop
to take pictures.
The mountains were not
tinted violet. The sunset
was never in the picture.
The man jumped
to the next outcrop.
Wearing sandals no less.
Happened so fast
I could not see.
A camera and tripod
over his left shoulder.
Only his right hand
to grip the rock.
His name remains
unknown. The face
was not visible.
The truth is
the image can lie
invisible for decades.
A ledge lies
just out of shot.
Everything depends on
molecules of vapor.

Mathew Brady Reflects on a Daguerreotype from Jackson's Last Year of Life

To make a daguerreotype,

     a silver surface must be mirror-polished.

The resulting image is negative,

    but the surface reflects the image

   to appear positive.

       The portrait will have no duplicates.

Therefore,
    a government should preserve its dead.

After years of living history,

      a face becomes a landscape of ghosts.
The end of a life   carries weight and line.

Time's mistakes:

  the face *and* the surface.

      Generating from the face itself,

(some fingerprints   and some fog)

  they conquer it.   A fortune rests in preserving lines,

lost eyes and names.

A man poses for preservation.   Dignity may fail in the lines.

Boulevard du Temple

A city apparently abandoned
except for a single man having his boots
polished—the first depiction
of human presence in a photograph
whose city street, closed off
by a neat line of trees,
rushes headlong
toward us—the composition alone
indicating movement—
but what we cannot see
is the motion—too fast
for early cameras, taking
too much time to expose—
carriages driving down the street,
like so many shopkeepers
hurrying beneath
the buildings' awnings to work;
and women carrying parasols,
having waited too long
on a summer day, dash
to buy dinner bread and wine;
and another man—entranced
by the music of a distant street
performer—whose shadows dance
off his Venetian blinds—all become
lost subjects in the photographer's rush
to capture this instant—while the single figure,
faceless and blurred—
poses with one foot raised,
still as polished marble
among the busyness
of the Paris boulevard.

Radiography

Hummingbirds shape smoke trails in the sky.

Beneath the ribs the heart remains whole,

and wasps have constructed paper cities there.

If we look inside the cranium,

we find a mapmaker's dream, gyri

become river systems. Networks of tubes

emerge onto the other side of the world.

Gondoliers row through the canals;

swarms of cabbage moths color the banks.

Originally, the X-ray technician

was called a skiagrapher: shadow writer.

Scientists who studied these rays

often died from exposure. Unlike sunburn,

radiation burns continue to expand outward

even after contact has ended, enveloping

larger sections of skin. Beneath the eyes,

a lighthouse beam: when we face,

the world radiates primary color.

Autochrome of a Mongolian Prisoner in a Box

An arm emerges.

A hole in the side.

Shadows < ... > hair.

Grasping a lock.

Color from tinted grains.

72,000 photographs—one of

< ... > is mostly   our view.
About entrapment.

If we look closely < ... >
of the face visible.

Microscopic potato starch. Definition from lampblack.

Endless steppes—
livestock, perhaps,
in the distance.

Can be viewed through handheld projector.

Spots of red, blue, and green where they should not.

Image on a mirror   ground glass.

< ... > the key.

Kirlian Photography

A fingerprint shines blue light
from each swirl's perimeter.

A leaf, even after it is torn,
will generate fluorescence

from the severed section. According
to Kirlian, this is the object's life source—

intrinsic energy the objects leave
on the photographic plate.

But a coin too gives light—residue
of its owner's perspiration,

which in turn makes the metal
more conductive. Or, a remnant

of the owner's skin. Perhaps even
energy from Jefferson's face

on the nickel. The body becomes an image
by crafting the shadow in light.

Newer photographies detect light
around their subjects through sensors

like those on a polygraph machine.
Movements pulse under the skin and manifest

their rhythms as different colors of light.
Each photograph's aura

depends on the moment it is taken.
Tonight, in the museum garden,

ghost tourists take pictures, the darkness
sparking like a lightning storm.

With proper flash and shutter speed,
the camera may reveal dust motes

through lamplight, wisps of vapor,
possible phantoms.

Memory

Two photographs: in one,
a buck stands at a wood's edge.
The grasses dried from early frosts
barb a fallen tree, a border
beyond which the animal looks,
hesitating to move.
A row of birches, a pine in the near distance.
The second is the same picture,
blurred. Colors fuse—
the beige grasses join with the fallen tree's bark.
Without focus, the deer flees
into the detritus. The buck's antlers
form new birches.

And in a twenty-first century funeral parlor,
a circle forms around the body.
A hundred flashes: the face rouged,
the hair styled and brushed,
nails painted red—
a final memento before cremation.
When the cell phone captures this moment,
there is room for error.
The dress's unfocused square designs,
the folded hands obscured by a flash
can be erased. No passage
through chemical baths before shape sets.
Years later, our memories
will conform to the images.
The animal still at nature's edge,
or sprinting into the black space.
The single, perfectly preserved body.
The photographer renders it,

mediates its passage
between this world and the next.

II. THE HUNTER'S MOON OVER CHICAGO

The Hunter's Moon over Chicago

1.

A fire long ago: the courthouse bell pealed
for miles throughout the city,
then crashed through the floors.
Everywhere, in fact, haunted—
the memory of the fire swarming
through oil slicks created by boats
and setting the river afire, running up
dock works and embankments, engulfing
wooden streets and sidewalks and buildings.
A city worker pumped water
from the Tower's highest floors
until the fire encroached upon the building.
When he saw the waterworks were ruined,
he jumped to his death to keep
from being consumed in flames.
These buildings have been reconstructed
from brick now, several times gutted and rebuilt
with hardwood floors and freshly painted walls.
Intertwining arcs of polished metal
stand on the site of the disaster's origin,
outside the fire academy.
Walking yesterday, I saw graffiti painted
on the underside of a bridge:
With the heat comes wanting.

2.

Tonight the full lunar eclipse, the hunter's moon—
the moon passes entirely inside
the Earth's shadow and turns bright red.
In my bedroom window, a candle burns in a pool
of its own wax, the wick so low
the flame hovers blue.
I watch its wavering in the glass,
watch the moon redden from the playground
across the street. In another time,
men hunted for the coming winter's food
by this light, the animals migrating into its fire.
There will be enough light to cast my shadow
under the streetlamps and across the wet leaves
decaying their sweet smell into the ground,
the fragrance rising through the playground jungle's
metal slides and bars. Every afternoon,
an old man comes here to exercise.
He rounds-off, makes a handstand, holds
his weight a minute, and falls upright.
Sometimes he removes his maroon sweater
in the heat worked up from moving
in short, swift pull-ups on the equipment.
When he finishes he walks slowly
to regain his breath, starts the cycle again.

3.

Winter comes quickly:
big snowflakes fall and melt
on asphalt. On the next bus to Little India,
I see the snow-brushed beaches
and the lakeshore tower constructed in cloverleaf
so all its residents can see the water,
but never into another's home.
A man drunk and eager to talk
moves from the back of the bus
to the seat next to mine.
He works as a cook, shows me his sliced
knuckles, tells how much he paid
to move here from Mexico.
When he reaches his stop, he extends
his scraped hand, wishes me the best.
Behind me, college students bundled in blue down coats
are talking about moving
into new apartments, carrying furniture
over curbs filled with plowed snow and slush.
They each exit, and I am the only one
left when the driver stops under a bridge
and tells me I have reached the end of the line.
On the train platform above the street,
shivering cold, I wait,
looking into the Laundromat below
where washers circle slowly, smearing
soap on glass. The patrons stare past their laundry,
the windows, so much water—
the Chicago River flowing into the Mississippi
flowing into the ocean.

4.

Someone has discarded a rose
on the beach. Only one side
of the corolla remains: the petals
dried and wine-red. Next to it,
a dead tree branch sprouts
from the sand—pieces of sea grass
hang like Spanish moss
from the limbs. I can feel
the sand between my toes,
even though I am wearing
both socks and shoes.
My clothes are seaweed:
I can feel every grain.

5.

The shells of zebra mussels cluster
in the sand. They are native to Europe's
inland seas, traveled so far on the sides
of ships like barnacles or in the mouths
of water birds. All the northern lakes
in the country are filled with them now.
They have formed piles here. On the pier,
a man is performing a dance: one foot
forward, a bend to the side, other foot
in front. He is not dancing, in fact;
he has no partner. I walk to the end
of the beach, and the man is at the pier's
edge, swaying as if bowing to the waves.
I walk back, and he has made a circle,
a slow waltz down the planks.
I must be the other dancer.

6.

On the corner, a street musician warms up,
plays a tinny backbeat too loud on a portable stereo,
something recorded years ago
and worn thin. He sits steps away from me
against the bus stop's glass.
As he begins, the air seems to warp
with the distortions on the tape, bending
the street concavely into the saxophone's bell,
swallowing the buildings
and everyone who stands waiting.
But before I can reach to pause
the cassette to stop the air's rupturing,
his reed splits. Below us, a crack
is forming in the glass. Sheets of newspaper
have collected at the bases of buildings.
All the wrong notes are slipping out.
Somehow, all this brokenness
stops time from swelling.

7.

In a darkened subway car we see each other's faces
in gasps—black, then pulses of form,
then black again. Above ground, a drain lends light
to the tunnel's carved concrete.
In the back of the car, a man
lowers his head in exhaustion.
Signs detail the distances
to surface exits, beams off metal
highlight words in advertisements,
a glint from a woman's eyeglasses
reveals the calluses on her hands.
When light returns, we trace
the outlines of faces, but close our eyes
so we may process each shape more slowly,
take time to comprehend the parts:
colors of shirts, books straightened in laps—
a way to read every expression.

8.

Concrete slabs along the beach's edge
display children's names painted
and chalked: totems from the rubble.
Perhaps these are surplus stones
from a nearby building, or a home
never finished, or a sidewalk poured to extend
underneath the sand and into the water,
a pier with nothing to fall from.
Even now, the path to the street seems to emerge
from the sand, fading from a billion particles
into the city. Flat rocks cover the beach
where I am walking now. These can be good to skip,
but can also serve as worry stones—objects to rub
between the fingers, to press until warmed,
as if the rock were formed between thumb
and forefinger. I choose one from the sand
to soften. This rock is not yet so smooth;
its pits and cavities make it feel
like pumice. With enough trouble,
I can craft an agate.

9.

About the insides of things—
in those drawbridges over the train yards,
rooms encased in glass—large enough
for someone to live should he want to make
the trip so high, balanced over air,
every day.   From such heights,
when streetlights burn and glare off car windows,
the city becomes an orange lattice.
From my window, my faint reflection
superimposes onto the bridge-room.
My face tarpaulin or edifice.

10.

In the natural science building,
a human skeleton too
fragile to be touched
hangs on a hook inside
a glass case. The bones
have yellowed,
and disintegrating ribs
have been replaced at their tips
with leather strands.
Looking down,
the lowest ribs
diminish as if broken.
Lengths of wire
string vertebrae together.
In the sternum,
a single screw.
Faint writing illegible
where the cranium
has been opened and
replaced like a jar lid.
At the other end
of the hallway, a window
reflects my body: knees
bent, elongated
in the glass. No face.

11.

Once, my apartment was a city politician's office.
In an archive somewhere,
there is a short film of him at work,
a film called "Favors." One by one,
district residents enter his office
to ask for a recommendation letter for a promotion.
A hole in the sidewalk, refilled without support
underneath, must be fixed. The concrete will not
hold, will sink if not reinforced.
Only so much can be done, we are told.
The film ends.

In my living room's worn red tile floor,
four white squares bear his monogram
like markings on a tomb.
When I moved in, my cat disappeared—
only to emerge two hours later
from a small rectangular hole under a cabinet.
Who knows where she had been
or what she found—some dusty tunnel long
abandoned except by the spiders or centipedes
occasionally emerging from cracks under walls.
Fissures in beams. Mortar eroding from masonry.
Some nails and a book. A small rodent's skeleton.
The blueprints sketched in sand.

12.

No power. In my living room, water is seeping
through the floor from a once-soldered pipe.
The only sounds come from the plumbing's bubbling:
rusting pipes straining against century-old joists.
I feel through the dark to the upstairs entryway
where my neighbor stands in the stairwell
as his nephew walks barefoot into the splash
under the building's canopy.
We watch the storm through the front door
and begin to talk about Spain. As a youth,
he attended a bullfight, became entranced
with the soldiers' military regalia—
in the sun, the brass shining:
on each button some type of emblem,
either coat of arms or lighthouse,
anchor or cornet. Golden insignias
attached to a yellow sash draped
over the jacket. A red feather standing
atop the hat so like the picadors' lances
in the ring. On the same trip,
he climbed the coastal mountains
near Málaga. Lost in the evergreens
thick around the rocks, he approached a cliff's edge
and nearly fell to his death.
With no humming air conditioners,
refrigerators, sodium street lamps,
our voices are louder than usual tonight.

In the morning, still no electricity.
At the storm's end, ninety thousand
lightning strikes: more than half a year's
lightning in one night. On the concrete,
leaves pressed down by hard rain

cast their afterimages
as if they had drifted into wet cement.
In my bathroom, a night light glows faintly.

13.

The sky has turned black, and the streets
are slicked with rain. In other rooms
of the office building,
the wind often blows through
window cracks. Here, the windows are sealed
shut; I cannot feel the air's force.
Across the street, in the interstate's cloverleaf,
cars make circles for new direction.
A train pulls in.
The grass rectangle turns to mud.

On July Fourth, I stood in that grass
hoping to see fireworks not obscured
by the city skyline or tall trees
surrounding the campus. There was no clear view
from Harrison Street, just an occasional
blue comet flying over the treetops.
Every explosion, though, I could feel.

14.

I walk down Ashland Avenue
on one of the summer's last nights.
Office windows blaze in a white building,
and all the pedestrians are speaking
languages I cannot understand.
At the corner, a Christian mission offers
blood tests from the back of a van.
Amid stacks of pamphlets teaching God's Word,
men sit on black upholstery, tubes taped to their arms,
their blood welling into the clinicians' vials.
Across the street a neon sign hangs
over a building's entryway, lights the name
of its first occupant over the lintel.
I see my face in a storefront window.
Once when I was very young, I looked
into a mirror, pointed to myself, and said
the wrong name. My mother believed
in reincarnation, said blue eyes suggest
ancient souls. But my eyes are not wholly blue.
The iris's inner rim is green.
And on certain days and with certain clothes,
they turn a shade of grey.
In my eyes, the city's language.

III. ARCHAEOACOUSTICS

Leavening

Something driven between: a beak.

A spring of teal and a troubling of goldfish.

Hair is feather, is scales. Your knuckles pressing the dough flat.

Sound of bells tolling: exaltation of larks.

Yeast in the water. Waves rise.

A siege of cranes. A mutation of thrushes.

Bread made with honey—drops of it in the center.

Straw floating in the rain—perhaps a hollow bone.

Yellow bread. A grist of bees.

A strand of your hair in my fingers. Nothing left but the dust.

A drop of honey, a knife, an empty plate on the counter.

A wedge of flying swans. Descent of woodpeckers.

Rain scours pollen from the ground. River of salt.

Learning Polish

You are thinking too much, trying to think
about it in English at the same time,
the instructor says. *Trzydzieści.*
I believe I may never be able to speak it either,
a necessary word. But this
is the only way for me:
assembling the sounds
together as in English, speaking quickly
only the consonants surrounding
the space between words—*not Zhivago.*
Repeat and try again. *Trzydzieści.* Thirty.
As in, soon I will be. I cannot
leave English behind now. *Przepraszam.*
Instead, English and Polish at once—
stop, Zhivago—listen to how
the consonants collapse together
over the space; everything else erased.
I have said it. *Przepraszam.* Repeat.
I'm sorry. *Szczęście.* Happiness.
Hush, Chad—the sound of calm,
said twice. Then, a cry of pain
before concluding again near silence. I repeat.
Szczęście. Repeat it. Happiness.

Archaeoacoustics

According to some stories, one can record sound into pottery—given something to mark grooves in the clay, a piece of straw or several fibers from a broom—while spinning it on a wheel. It may be possible, with the proper equipment, to hear the voice of the craftsman on unearthed shards.

A fork run across china.   You say to me, *hold.*

Chalk on a blackboard.   I hear, *gone.*

A car braking: a sharp turn.   You say to me, *cold.*   Ghost voices.

Sounds like, *heart.*   Watchworks turning.   I hear,

choose.   A child dragging a stick on the ground.   You say to me,

carve.   The stylus skipping against   the record's label.

You say to me,   *hand.*   A swing on a playground

in the middle of the night. Sounds like, *him.*   Water spinning

down a drain.   You say to me, *feel.*   *Freeze.*

Hymn.   *Heal.*   *Cord.*   *Home.*   .   *Fail.*

Lexicon

Llorar. 1. Yurt: houses made of skin.

2. Yearning: even under the umbrella, you cry.

Deszcz. 1. Dust: cobwebs, scraps of paper—all of it swept into the corners.

2. Etch: acid rain.

Reißen. 1. Ricebird: the male's yellow crest like a sunflower in the field.

2. Risen: the oven filled with bread.

Déchirer. 1. Dishcloth: water dripping down your hands when wrung.

2. Decay: the leaves in the gutter, thick and heavy with rain.

Pleurer. 1. Pleura: breath rises over the lungs.

2. Plural: making the nouns agree—so many of them.

Pleuvoir. 1. Plovers, falling.

2. Oeuvre: the house we have built, what rests inside it.

Krzyczeć. 1. Crashes: termites in the joists; dust raining from their holes in the wood.

2. Czardas: the dance begins slowly, but finishes as a typhoon.

Drżeć. 1. Drench: covered in rain.

2. Judge: what we have finished will define us.

Schreien. 1. Shriven: confession—we tell each other everything.

2. Shrine: in silence, watching the candles die.

L/over.   1. Love: the ovenbird builds its nest over us.

2. You've: Please, this you can keep.

Archives

In Russia's medieval Zvenigorod, drivers cannot see
from the highway the Cathedral of the Assumption,
obscured between a mountain and river, by heavy
rows of firs and spruces, a line of gorges.
The cupola's golden cross emerges just above
the horizon. Early architects aimed
to create illusions about the cathedral's size. They
broke symmetry: pillars were moved, the chancel
and apses broadened, kokoshniks carved around the
dome, intricate masonry built for the frame.
The birth of a prince occasioned a new building,
military wins led to a new bell tower. Now for years,
a geometry of scaffolding and netting has lined the perimeter.
Art restorers repairing the walls have since found
fragments of prophets and holy leaders concealed
beneath layers of paint on the dome drum's walls:
scenes from St. John the Baptist's life. More series of frescos,
mostly likely by painter-saint Andrei Rublev, were unearthed
behind the iconostasis. Most recently, archaeologists
discovered elaborate birds' nests in the attic, formed from
letter scraps written in the elaborate calligraphy of tsarinas,
rubles, beak-torn documents, branches, skulls of cats
and other birds, stamps and fragments of sealing wax.
A discarded nineteenth century candy wrapper illustrates
the sun from a tarot deck. A cigarette carton with images
from a painting. Ration cards from the Stalin era.
An intertwined pastiche of the town: petals of butterfly weed,
dried elephant ear, wafer ash, mineral paint fragments,
weeping honey locust, purple birch, eggshell slivers,
a shard of green glass, spiderwebs, jewels of opar,

yarn cuttings and grass cuttings, pine cones.
In the church, an icon, reputed to work miracles—
curing the ill, answering prayers for the sick and weary,
saving the town from enemy raids during the Great
Patriotic War. In this place, Rublev also painted *Christ as Saviour.*
His Christ, peaceful and impossibly tall, gazes directly
into the viewer's eyes. From his hair, which has peeled entirely
into a ghosted halo, decay runs in rivers down his face, into his garment.

St. Catherine of Alexandria and the Red Sea

The captain of a Red Sea ferry [the Saint Catherine] has admitted he steered clear of a doomed ship that sank between Saudi Arabia and Egypt with the loss of about 1,000 lives to avoid a "second catastrophe." —Agence France Presse

We have not these acts in their original form.

Lamp light burns in the oratory: bush fire.

On the water, fire burns for hours. The captain turned away.

Transformed and distorted by fantastic and diffuse descriptions.

In angels' hands, her fragile body carried to the mountain top.

The glass ruins of the office. The windowpane an empty spider web.

Two rescued by boat. A man and a boy.

The imagination of the narrators.

Shards flying from the wheel: wood spikes.

Crowds gather at the ambulance window.

To charm their readers by recitals of the marvelous. Who cared less.

The monastery now a fortress to ward off Saracens. Conversion.

A row of policemen dressed in black. The crowd throws rocks.

Invested with a halo of charming poetry and miraculous power.

A tire, a mound of stones. Fire burning in the circle.

Glass Harmonica

Ladies and gentlemen, running
moistened fingers around these goblets' rims
fashions music nearly vocal
and with the echoes of a rung bell.
This instrument goes by many names:
seraphim, ghost fiddle, and finally,
hydrodaktulopsychicharmonica:
roughly translated, harmonica music
made for the soul by dipping fingers
in water. Mesmer used it to test his theories
of animal magnetism. Benjamin Franklin
designed one with rims colored
according to pitch. Some musicians
were rumored to have been poisoned
by playing the lead-coated glass.
A German musicologist noted
the glass harmonica *excessively stimulates*
the nerves, plunges the player
into a nagging depression and hence
into a dark and melancholy mood
that is apt for slow self-annihilation.
My friends, how about a wager:
what happens to the sound when I remove
water from the glass? Does the pitch
increase or decrease?   In the Mississippi Delta,
a string of islands has been obliterated,
a lighthouse toppled; sand and sediment
will not be restored. In the French Quarter,
gutters pump rain into the streets,
and ferns drip from balconies.

On Magazine Street, a family's century-old house
is collapsing—rooms filled with mazes
of paper-filled boxes and rusted furniture.
Just one cigarette, and the house could go up
like kindling, ignite the entire block.
The siblings are elderly and mentally ill.
They must move. In the aquatic gardens,
a groundskeeper wades into the ponds,
holds up water lilies; last year's plantings
have flourished. With his hands,
he cleans anacharis grass
from the water beds. And now
ladies and gentlemen, let us return to the glass.
You will notice when water is removed,
the pitch increases. Encyclopedias of musicology
have these facts all wrong. But the circles
my hands make tell no lies.
As your airplane circled for landing
over Lake Pontchartrain, you saw from your window
the world's longest bridge, cars driving
into fog. Tell me, what happens
when the clouds over the lake swallow you up?

Liquidity

1.

Up for auction: a Greentown Glass
chocolate sawtooth dolphin candy dish

with fish top. Authentic:
ten teeth on each side

of the mouth. The depression
inside the dish follows

the tail's curve. Manufacturing cracks
near the mouth: remnants of the cooling process.

Once, barrelsful sold for nickels apiece—
the cost of a bread loaf.

Green drinking glasses were hidden
incentives in oat and detergent boxes,

punch bowls and cups free
with oil changes. Prices, of course,

fluctuate—check a catalog for appraisal.
The dolphin today—

two thousand dollars, starting price.
Hold up your placard and make a bid.

Next: a cobalt blue cord drapery
cruet, then heirloom amethyst candle holders.

Collectors must confirm quality. Note
that not all pieces will sell at auction.

In my mother's cabinet, a clear cake pedestal,
inherited from her great-grandmother.

A true antique, over a century old.
Be sure to check for bubbles

or molding marks. Families ate from these
pieces daily—look for utensil scratches.

Run a finger around the rim;
feel for chips. Avoid so-called sick glass

clouded by automatic dishwashers.
Evaporation rings can be removed;

lost luster is permanent.
Mother had assumed

the cake pedestal would carry value. On its surface,
bubbles rise from the base.

The pattern is neither clearly
floral nor geometric. Looked at from above,

its honeycombs, or leaves, radiate
to the center, then whirlpool

out at the stand
eventually dissolving to nothing.

2.

Questions arise. How to account
for the discrepancies?

Certain glass may break
like a solid, but will flow

like a liquid if left on a table for a week.
A physicist deems it *a supercooled liquid.*

Other scientists claim the thickness
of antique windows' bases

demonstrates that glass is liquid,
melting slowly over centuries

in cathedral panes. But if this were true,
we should also see pooling

in medieval telescopes, ancient Egyptian figurines.
When the blower spins the glass,

the edges are thicker. When mounting,
workers placed the panes

thick side down to stabilize them,
to prevent water from accumulating

in the lead cames at the base.
When windows are carelessly installed,

we find the thick side top-up.
In recent factory productions,

we see similar effects: where glass is emptied
on cooling tables to spread, it is always thicker

where it was poured. We deleted *frozen*
from the physicist's words.

The professor said, *Glass is a liquid
which has lost the ability to flow.*

3.

No records left—the factory destroyed.
The fire unexplained. The natural gas reserves

suddenly run dry. With nothing
to fire the furnaces, the operation was finished.

No one replicated the molds.
The company's president

confiscated the family glass formulas.
A museum was opened

on the sixty-seventh anniversary of the fire.
Visitors can see the remaining

blue agate spooner there,
or the Holly Amber series,

the only one recognized
by the Museum of Modern Art.

Another exhibit explains how to tell
genuine productions from fakes.

This factory created designs in unusual colors—
emerald green, teal, canary yellow, cobalt.

No manufacturing records remain—
new letterhead soon announces

a chocolate glass orange tree hairpin holder.
In replicas, pinks may appear

shades darker, even orange.
Weight and thickness are key—

the glass becomes heavier with time.
Cookie jar handles sometimes

elongate, sharpen at the edges.
Look for utensil scratches—an indication

of authenticity. Some plates, when stacked,
should form a letter V:

an optical illusion. Experts researching paintings
have discovered methods for eliminating

visual guesswork—X-ray and infrared technology,
chemical pigment analyses. A hair from

Jackson Pollock's balding head lodged in the paint
can be matched to DNA in his studio.

Don't be misled, however:
probability may still best determine

composition dates. In this trade,
there can be no certainty.

4.

At a party in Boston,
the family poured an inferior Chablis

into the crystal, but all in attendance
remarked on its sweetness.

The husband stood by his wife's side.
She recalled a story to the guests

in which she had walked to the pond
on her family's estate

one summer day in her childhood.
Before she reached its bank,

she'd caught her dress on a low briar.
Unaware, she leaned toward the water

and heard the fabric tear.
At that moment, something in her broke—

she imagined being told her parents died
and she would be forced to live

in a faraway orphanage. She ran home
crying and could not stop until

her mother held her and she fell
asleep through her tears.

To that day, she said,
she could not stand the sound

of anything tearing, not even a piece of paper.
The guests looked into their glasses

and drank the wine. They did not know
the harm of ingesting so little.

When the husband lay on his deathbed
a few years later, a nurse dropped a camphor bottle,

the fumes dissipating throughout the room.
At that moment, she thought she heard him:

I cannot bear the sound
of breaking glass—cannot bear—

5.

In the Gulf of Mexico, archaeologists
date to the War of 1812

this unnamed ship's wreck. It carried
perfectly preserved telescopes, hourglasses, compasses,

buttons, pieces of a pocket watch.
The objects are measured with lasers,

labeled on maps, assigned unique bin numbers.
Mustard jars embossed *LONDON*

match jars from another site—
the word and image allow

scientists to estimate the ship's age.
Still, we do not know its origin,

its destination. For simplicity's sake,
newspapers call it the Mardi Gras Shipwreck.

We assume we will find answers in the ordering,
though we still need measurements for the losses:

where the magnets would have pointed,
which comet lost to its observer,

on whose mantel a timepiece would be placed.
In the depths, slipping sand

mimics the ocean's sweep in soft tides.
Sunken to the ocean floor over two centuries ago,

the telescopes' leather cases
have survived intact. The same cannot be said

for the ship's cannon—the original iron
has degraded to such a degree

that only the organisms residing inside
hold it together when lifted from the water.

Washing Wine Glasses

What has been left behind
gathers in small pools.
Residue of grapes
grown on New Zealand mountains
in the basins of dry, ancient rivers.
Every drop lingers
on the glass, stains it red.
I run a dishcloth over the outside,
gently roll the rag up and clean the interior.
In the sink, it is often difficult to tell
the difference between soap
and flaws in the glass. I move my finger
across the rim and listen. A killdeer:
the ring around its eye. Pyrrhuloxia.
Rinse, and pink water empties.
My hand's reflection is a barrel of French oak,
and the lines of my palm are rivers.

Recordings of Dead Languages

Alexander von Humboldt followed
a Venezuelan river to find the Orinoco's source.
Along a certain rain forest trail,
he encountered a group of Carib Indians
who had recently killed a tribe
of neighboring Maypurés. Among their plunders,
the Caribs had taken some parrots.
During the encounter, the birds
spoke some Maypuré words, which von Humboldt
recorded in his journal. The parrots spoke
the names of lilies, a cranesbill,
a type of piranha. Von Humboldt saw trees
he could not identify. *Moriche palm.*
It is called the tree of life, they said.
What is this? von Humboldt asked.
Condor. This is the name.
Caracas, hoatzin, macaw,
iguana, chapurro, toucan.
This is what they are called.
They croaked these words and a scribe
wrote them as best he could.
The birds flew into the canopies
and called behind them. *Oilbird.*
Manganese. Flamingo. Capybara.
The parrots traveled and traveled.
freeing words as they blended
into the greenery.

Notes

"Recognition" is after Jeff Wall's *Flooded Grave* (1998-2000).

The poem "Tell the Bees" is after and takes its title from the exhibit "Tell the Bees... Belief, Knowledge and Hypersymbolic Cognition" at the Museum of Jurassic Technology.

The sources of the lines in "After the End of the World: Centos" are as follows:

1. *The Drought*, J.G. Ballard; *The Road*, Cormac McCarthy; *The Handmaid's Tale*, Margaret Atwood; *The Dispossessed*, Ursula K. LeGuin; *On the Beach*, Nevil Shute; *We*, Yevgeny Zamyatin; *The Iron Heel*, Jack London; *The Drowned World*, J.G. Ballard; *Fahrenheit 451*, Ray Bradbury; *The Death of Grass*, John Christopher; *The Stone Gods*, Jeanette Winterson; *The Lathe of Heaven*, Ursula K. LeGuin; *Alas, Babylon*, Pat Frank.

2. *The Drowned World*; *Panther in the Hive*, Olivia Cole; *The Man in the High Castle*, Philip K. Dick; *The Death of Grass*; *The Age of Miracles*, Karen Thompson Walker; *The Handmaid's Tale*; *American War*, Omar el-Akkad; *Never Let Me Go*, Kazuo Ishiguro; *Parable of the Sower*, Octavia Butler.

3. *Oryx and Crake*, Margaret Atwood; *Alas, Babylon*; *American War*; *The Lathe of Heaven*; *The Hunger Games*, Suzanne Collins; *Brave New World*, Aldous Huxley; *The Plot Against America*, Philip Roth; *The Death of Grass*; *1984*, George Orwell; *Children of Men*, P.D. James.

4. *American War*; *Fahrenheit 451*; *Never Let Me Go*; *The Man in the High Castle*; *A Canticle for Leibowitz*, Walter M. Miller; *Darkness at Noon*,

Arthur Koestler; *The Stone Gods*; *Dub Steps*, Andrew Miller; *1984*; *The Handmaid's Tale*; *Station Eleven*, Emily St. John Mandel.

5. *On the Beach*; *Panther in the Hive*, Olivia Cole; *Station Eleven*; *Darkness at Noon*; *A Canticle for Leibowitz*; *Super Sad True Love Story*, Gary Shteyngart; *The Handmaid's Tale*; *The Dispossessed*; *The Man in the High Castle*; *Cat's Cradle*, Kurt Vonnegut; *Galapagos*, Kurt Vonnegut.

Several of the poems in "The Latent Image" were inspired by a variety of sources:

The second section of "Grand Canyon Triptych" is after Laws's "Trans-Canyon Telephone Line Construction - Silouette [sic] of CCC Enrollee Attaching Wire to Pole at the Edge of a Steep Cliff near the Rim" (ca. 1935) from the Grand Canyon National Park Museum Collection, and the third section is after Hans Van de Vorst's "Grand Canyon Leap 2" (2008).

Section 2 is after a daguerreotype of Andrew Jackson from Mathew Brady's studio (1844 or 1845-- Library of Congress, Prints and Photographs Division, LC-USZC4-1807).

Section 3 is after Louis Daguerre's "Boulevard du Temple" (1832).

Section 4 is after Robin Monique Rios's *Observations Series* (2005-2008).

Section 5 is after Stéphane Passet's "Mongolian Prisoner in a Box" (1913—Musée Albert Kahn).

"Archives" is after the article "Discovery in a Cathedral Attic Suggests Birds Are the Best Archivists" by Claire Voon.

Italicized lines from "St. Catherine of Alexandria and the Red Sea" are from *The Catholic Encyclopedia*. The epigraph is from the article "Captain Refused to Help Red Sea Ferry" (February 7, 2006).

The italicized section of "Glass Harmonica" comes from Friedrich Rochlitz's *Musikalische Zeitung* (1798).

Acknowledgements

I would like to thank Christina Pugh, Jennifer Ashton, Ann Feldman, John Huntington, and Alex Kurczaba for their invaluable support, assistance, and advice. I would especially like to thank Garrett Brown whose multiple careful readings and comments helped these poems find their current forms. Thanks also go to Tasha Fouts, Ixta Menchaca Rosa, Srikanth Reddy, Jennifer Moore, Matthew Corey, and Anne Winters for their feedback. Finally, special thanks go to RD Morgan and Snežana Žabić for believing in this collection and giving it a permanent home.

I would finally like to thank the editors of the following journals where some of the poems in this collection were published, sometimes in a different version or with a different title: *Cream City Review, Faultline, Fifth Wednesday, Hamilton Stone Review, Literary Bohemian, Packingtown Review, In Other Words, Konundrum Engine Literary Review,* and *Offcourse.*

.

About the Author

Chad Heltzel earned his M.F.A. in Creative Writing at Texas State University, and his Ph.D. in English at the University of Illinois at Chicago. His poems have been published in *Faultline*, *Cream City Review*, *Fifth Wednesday*, and *Packingtown Review*, among other journals. He currently lives and teaches in Denver, Colorado.

www.ingramcontent.com/pod-product-compliance
Lightning Source LLC
Chambersburg PA
CBHW051326120626
46547CB00015B/2417